OVER THE BACK FENCE:

Learning Nature in a Bygone Napa Valley

A Natural History Memoir

By Douglas L. Murray

Sarco Creek near author's childhood home

Photo by Craig Philpott

Ideas into Books®
W E S T V I E W
P.O. Box 605
Kingston Springs, TN 37082
www.publishedbywestview.com

ISBN 978-1-62880-205-4 Perfect bound
ISBN 978-1-62880-206-1 Case laminate

First edition, August 2020

Cover and title page photo of Sarco Creek and Little Trancas Bridge page 24 — Photography copyright © 2020 Craig Philpott Photography, used
 with permission.
Family photographs and photo of early morning dew on page 48 courtesy of the author.
All other photos from Bigstockphoto.com.

Good faith efforts have been made to trace copyrights on materials included in this publication. If any copyrighted material has been included
 without permission and due acknowledgment, proper credit will be inserted in future printings after notice has been received.

Printed in the United States of America on acid free paper.

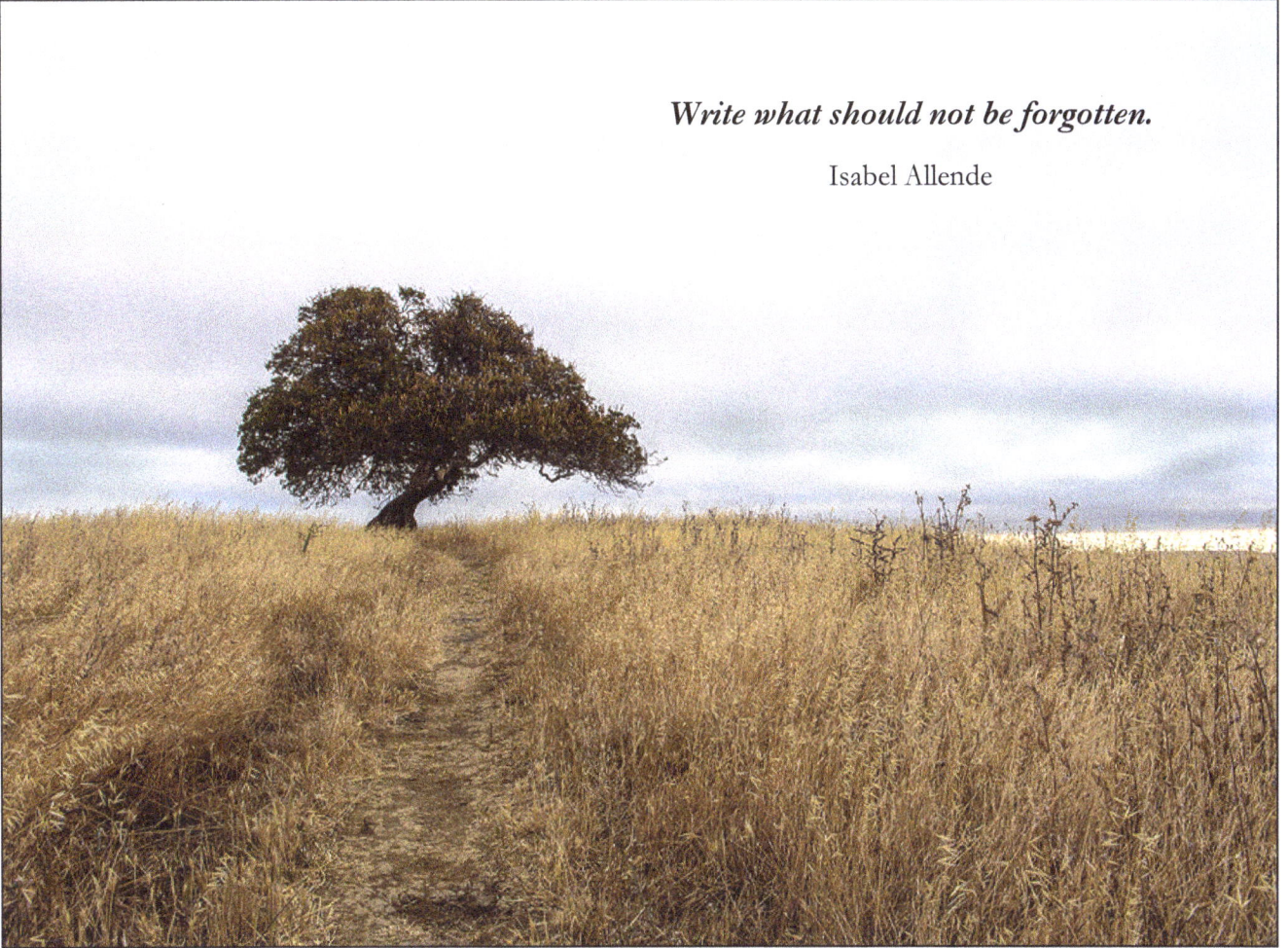

Write what should not be forgotten.

Isabel Allende

When one turns to telling their story they often proceed as if their life runs like a single thread from beginning to end. But upon reflection, one soon discovers that life is many stories intertwined, the warp and weft of many threads becoming an elaborate tapestry. In the telling of these stories one often finds them folding and unfolding, at times bending back upon themselves like Einstein's notion of time moving through a multi-dimensional universe. Still, the weaver of the most intricate fabric must begin with a single thread.

This is my recollection of my childhood and youth as a courtship with the natural world as I found it on the fringes of the Napa Valley from the 1950s to the mid-1970s. There are other threads to my life of course. A social one, not unlike the story told by my childhood friend Ray Guadagni in his book, *The Adventures of the Squeezebox Kid*. There is also the more traditional professional one, mine not worthy of comparison with innumerable wonderful stories of artists, political leaders and others told most frequently in biographical and autobiographical form. But for me the defining story of my life, the anchoring thread, emerges from a childhood spent in exploration and celebration of nature.

PART 1

A Free Range Childhood

My family moved to Napa when I was four. My parents were of that generation that grew up in the rural heartland but fled the hardships of agrarian life with the onset of the Great Depression, which ravaged rural America nearly a decade before it became a defining feature of what Tom Brokaw described as The Greatest Generation. Their generation moved first to nearby towns and then following the Second World War to urban centers, in this case the San Francisco Bay Area where my dad mustered out of the Navy at War's end. I was born in Berkeley in 1947 as was my sister four years later.

Like many of their generation, my parents longed for the middle class dream just beginning to take shape in post war society. The south end of Napa was where my family's quest brought them in 1951. We lived briefly in half of a duplex across the highway from the KVON Drive Inn Theater. My only memories of that time were of sneaking over to the bedroom window late at night to watch far off images of cowboys on horseback dashing across the screen with guns blazing, soldiers engaged in fierce combat in far off jungles, and tough-guy heroes gazing emotionless from the screen as beautiful heroines stared back longingly. Triumphal postwar Americana in all its glory, absent the sound.

We soon moved into town, renting the upstairs half of a two-story house from a local meat market owner, Steve Guisti, on Sycamore Street two blocks east of the Food City Market. My memories of that time were nearly as sketchy as they were of the previous residence. Visits to the nearby Fuller Park, a brief kindergarten stint at Shearer Elementary School, wandering around the immediate neighborhood, and not much else.

Then my parents bought a house when I was about five where my life and many of my foundational memories unfolded over the ensuing decade and a half. We moved to a transitional area in northeastern Napa between disconnected suburban developments and the rural regions of the Napa Valley, on Woodside Drive off Monticello Road. Our house was located on a dead-end street with a dozen or so other houses. Beyond our backyard fence my world opened onto a large fruit orchard of perhaps thirty acres, although it seemed as vast as a county to a five- or six-year-old, bordered to the south by another sixteen acres of open fields seasonally devoted to grazing sheep. It was the property of an old hermit and rancher, Louis Gasser, who would intermittently run me out of his orchard or in turn invite me to climb up on the two mule-drawn buck board wagon he rode around his ranch for as long as I lived there. The southern border of Gasser's Ranch was marked by Sarco Creek. It was exploring those orchards, fields and creek beyond my backyard fence that became the defining feature of my Napa Valley childhood.

****

A child left to his own devices and a certain degree of opportunity will invent worlds unique to and known only by himself. There were other children my age on our street, in this case three brothers, Tom, Jim and Rick Reid. We played football, basketball and baseball together in various lots and yards around the neighborhood, and fought each other on occasion, at least until the two closest to my age followed in their older brother's footsteps and grew into All-Conference college football players, a linebacker and defensive end no less. I was of average size as a six-year-old but grew slowly, eventually reaching the grand stature of about 5 foot 9 inches, while the neighbor kids transformed seemingly overnight into Incredible Hulks. Not surprisingly I grew out of fighting at a relatively early age, which is to say I survived my childhood. Although we were friends and spent a considerable amount of our childhood together, I gravitated in those early years toward spending much of my time alone. When I had the chance, I would invariably go over the back fence and head into open territories, a whole world unto myself.

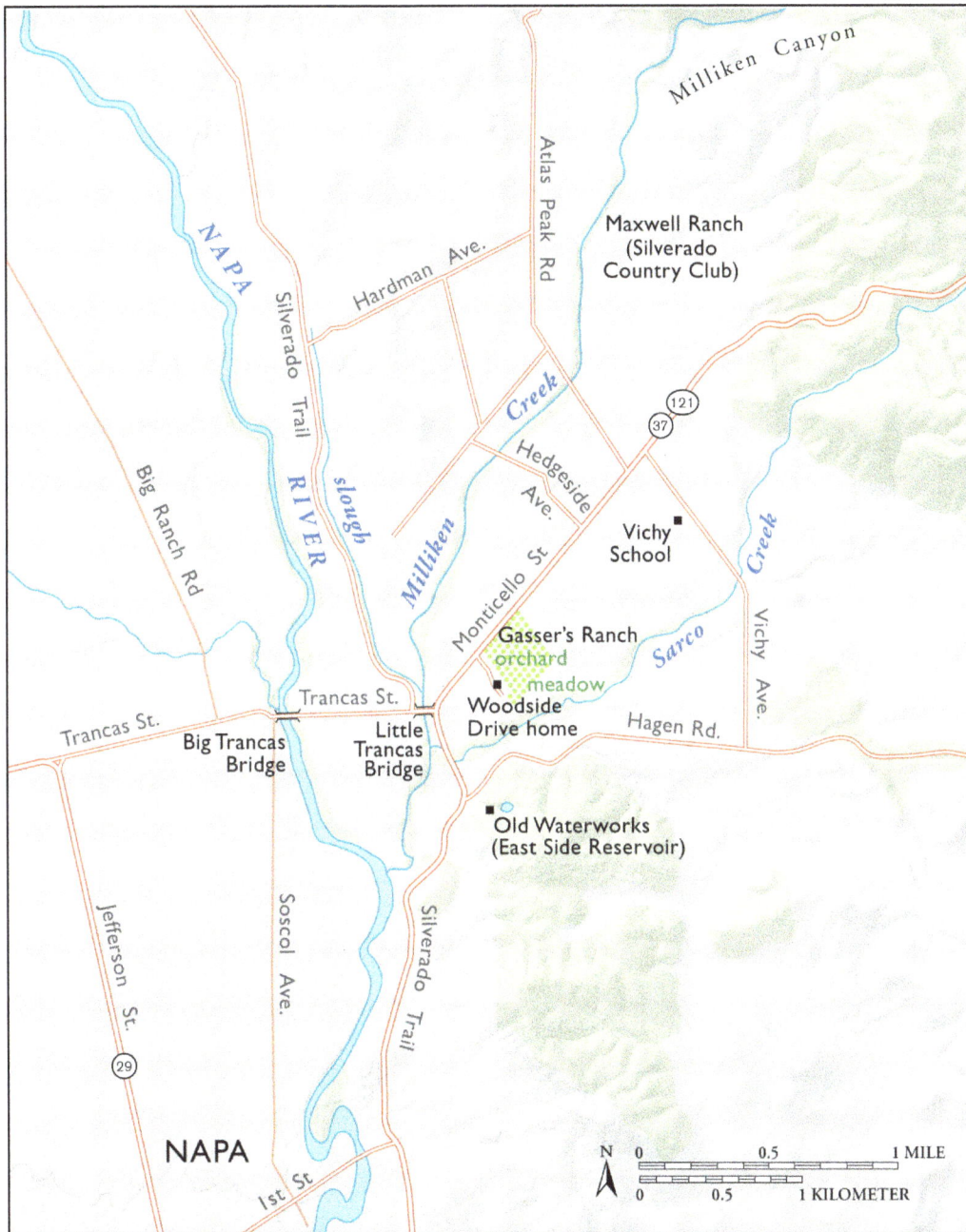

The orchard was an endless sea of French and Sugar plum trees, or what everyone called prunes. By late summer the trees were laden with purple fruit so heavy the branches had to be propped up with eight-to-twelve-foot-long stakes to keep the trees from splitting off large portions of their limbs. Deer would wander into the orchard to eat fallen fruit. Jack rabbits the height of a medium sized dog would dash erratically away as I wandered down the precisely spaced rows. Many kinds of birds flew about and chattered in the treetops – robins, red-headed finches, English sparrows, scrub jays, red-headed woodpeckers, mockingbirds, mourning doves and more. I came to know them as much by their songs as their colors and movements in flight.

To the south of the orchard was a small vineyard. Again, in the late summer I would wander down to the vines in search of the perfect cluster of grapes. Most of the vines were Concord or "slip skin" grapes destined for the table grape market or to one of the valley wineries like Krug, Beringer or Inglenook to be made into Burgundy wine or perhaps sacramental wine by the Christian Brothers. They were full of seeds and not particularly sweet. But scattered in amongst the red grapes were a few vines of white grapes. These were Muscats. They too were quite seedy, but they had the most exquisite sweet flavor, particularly the bunches that had turned yellow with a bronze hue to their upside where the sun had burnt them. Muscats are the oldest cultivated grape in the world. The Romans carried Muscat vines during the conquests to be planted throughout their empire. The table grapes one finds in today's supermarkets are mostly seedless hybrids. In the process of creating the generic white grape, that special flavor I sought out in the Muscat of Gasser's vineyard has been bred nearly into extinction. On rare occasions I have found grapes from Chile or Argentina in the supermarkets during winter that still have a hint of that long-forgotten Muscat. One taste and I am back on Gasser's ranch.

Further south on my daily trek through the ranch I would cross a large meadow. Most days I would flush a western meadowlark or two from the tall grass as I rambled southward. Their song is one of the most distinctive calls of the avian world and to this day when I hear the meadowlarks in the late spring on the ranch in Northern Colorado where I now live, I am again transported to that meadow of my childhood. But the real treasure of my summer wanderings south through Gasser's Ranch was Sarco Creek, which marked the property's southern boundary. As creeks go it wasn't much to talk about. By late summer it had almost stopped running. The creek bed was always in deep shadows as scrub oaks arched cathedral-like over the shallow stream. The daytime temperature in August often went well into the 90s but down beside the creek it remained cool and damp. Sunlight filtered through the dense overstory, casting gorgeous shades of greens, browns, yellows, and late in the day, soft blues as patches of the evening sky reflected off nearly motionless waters. There were clear pools in various stretches along the creek, mostly fed by underground springs. Here I would find a magical array of life. Inch long trout and other fry, small turtles and salamanders with leathery brown backs and orange bellies as bright as the citrus fruit.

In smaller more ephemeral pools where the green moss had taken over, I would find long translucent strands beneath the water's surface with black dots strung like beads along a clear thin necklace. Looking more closely I could see some of the beads occasionally wiggle. The next time I would venture down to those pools the small beads had hatched into tadpoles or what we called pollywogs, the black dots becoming little bodies propelled by tiny tails. With each subsequent visit the tadpoles would evolve, first sprouting tiny filaments where their tails joined their bodies and then similar frills closer to their heads, both soon becoming tiny limbs with even tinier fingers. Then eyes would appear framing a small mouth as the tails shortened and the tadpoles grew. Then one day upon my arrival a frenzy of frogs no larger than my thumb nail would jump into the mossy pool or scurry under the leaves along the bank.

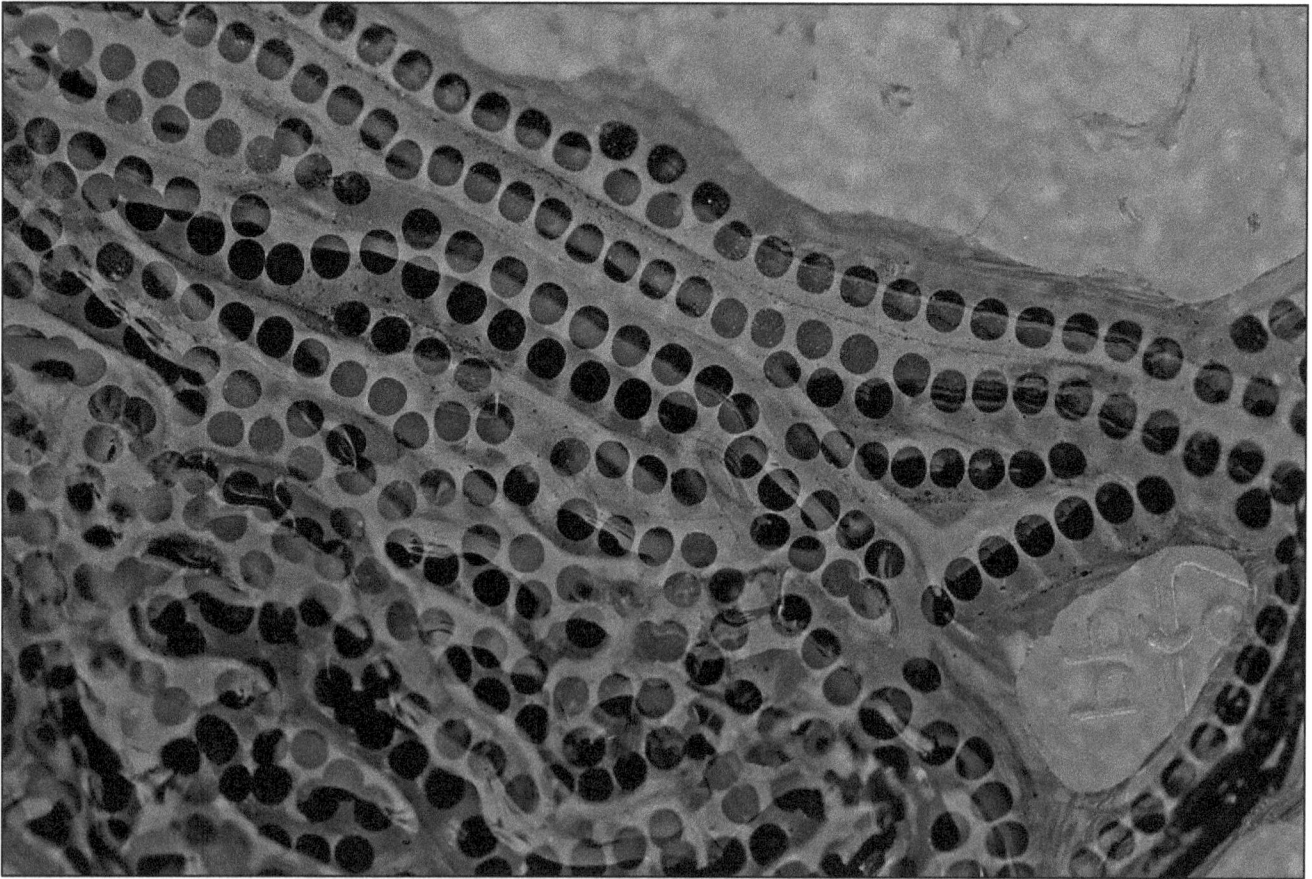

Some of the most exciting denizens of the summer creek bed were snakes. Garter snakes, with yellow stripes and sometimes red and blue side bands running the length of their bodies, would slide quickly into the underbrush or across a pool. Occasionally I would spot the tan markings of bigger gopher snakes tucked in under the roots of a tree along the bank. But most spectacular of all were the black and white banded king snakes. These were truly the most wondrous creatures. Some would reach lengths well over four feet. They were not aggressive, nor were they welcoming to a child's touch. They were best appreciated from a short distance. Sometimes I would just squat on the ground a few feet away and watch a large king snake. It would stare back for a time, flicking its tongue at me, then glide effortlessly back into the undergrowth as if to say, nice visiting with you but I have more pressing matters to attend to than a gawking little freckle faced kid. There were also rattlesnakes around, but I guess fortunately I never encountered one. Knowing they were about, as my parents and others warned, made the suspense of my nature hunts all-the-more exciting. There were also the unpleasant encounters with poison oak and stinging nettles which I experienced repeatedly in those early years until I became a little more cautious in what I touched, crawled through or brushed by.

I would lose myself for entire afternoons down in the creek. On occasion I would be so oblivious to the passing of time that I would all-of-a-sudden hear the onset of crickets and frogs chirping all around me. One moment silence, the next a symphony of invisible creatures calling forth the night. I would look up, sensing before fully realizing, that the sun was setting low in the sky, and I was in big trouble. Dad would be home from work by now and mom would be waiting for my return before setting dinner on the table. I would bolt across the meadow, over the fence into the vineyard and then through the orchard, finishing with a vault over the backyard fence and up onto the back porch. Panting and sweating, I would predictably be met by mom's scowl and orders to get washed up, followed by the inevitable lecture over dinner — if Tarzan cannot make it home in time for dinner, then maybe he should forego the jungle and stay in his room tomorrow afternoon. I sat with my eyes downcast, the epitome of the chastened supplicant. Yet internally I was hardly distraught as I had recently discovered books, short novels with wolves and mountain lions as the lead characters. So those days I found myself in lock down in my room I easily lost myself in the exploits of some of nature's most exciting and, at least in the telling of their stories, most charismatic of creatures.

****

Within several years of the discovery of my own magical aviary, the orchard beyond my back fence lost much of its allure as it became my first place of employment. Each fall the local schools would delay opening until the prune harvest was completed so grade school kids could be recruited into cheap, grueling farm labor. I spent long days on hands and knees filling buckets with plump, sticky prunes picked from the rough ground after trees had been shaken to drop the ripened fruit. Half bushel wooden lug boxes were filled from the buckets and hoisted onto Old Man Gasser's mule drawn wagon. Trucks full of the roughly 30-pound boxes of prunes would be delivered at the end of each day to one of the local commercial driers. Each week we were paid by the box for our efforts. The idea I suppose was to instill an appreciation of hard work at a young age, child labor laws notwithstanding. Not sure it ever achieved that lofty goal. Most of those days it merely led me to endless hours with aching knees, longing for my afternoons down in the shady coolness of Sarco Creek.

During that same period, somewhere around age 9, my best friend in grade school, Bruce Guthrie, invited me along with his grandfather, Pop Guthrie, to go fishing. We drove to Lake Hennessey, the reservoir behind Conn Dam some 20 miles or so up the east side of the valley. Pop took us to a short dock that stuck about 15 feet out in the lake next to the top of the spillway. Equipped with a cane pole, cork bobber, and a worm on a hook, I dropped the fishing line into the brownish clear water and the world below came alive. Small fish, mostly bluegill ranging in size from a couple of inches to the size of a man's hand, dashed to the baited hook. The bobber danced and plunged. I pulled up and a small bluegill was flipping madly on the end of my line. The grins, the excitement, the frenzied scramble as I hurriedly rebaited my hook and dropped it in again, testified to the significance of this new discovery. I was about to become a life-long fisherman.

After catching a couple more, the action slowed down. My gaze wandered across the lake to the rolling grass-covered hillsides spotted with manzanita, scrub oak and occasionally by the massive live oak trees for which the Napa Valley was famous. Waterfowl skittered over the lake's glassy surface while a great blue heron stood motionless just down the shoreline, stalking the very same fish we were dropping into our bucket. Pop Guthrie at one point leaned over my shoulder and said, "Hey daydreamer! Where's your bobber?" Sure enough, another fish had taken the hook while my imagination wandered. Daydreamer became a moniker that stuck with me throughout my childhood, and some would say still to this day.

That evening Pop dropped me off in front of our house. I marched onto the back porch with the bucket of fish and proudly presented what I was sure was a most incredible bounty. I expected mom and dad to cheer in celebration of my new-found prowess. Instead it was a moment for one of life's first bitter lessons. Mom peered into the bucket of a dozen or so bluegill, looked up at me and said, "OK Buster, you catch em, you clean em," then pivoted and walked away with another of her famous scowls. Dad, with a sigh, explained in his most paternal way that mom had grown up in a household of two older brothers and a father who fished and hunted every waking hour they were not at work on the oil rigs or railroad around their home in Laramie, Wyoming. She and her sisters would be sent to the mud porch when the men arrived home, usually after dark, with a stringer of fish or ducks or geese. The girls were expected to gut the fish, pluck and gut the ducks and geese, while the men had a couple of beers before their mom put dinner on the table. My mom made it clear to dad that cleaning game was not part of what she signed up for once she had escaped her childhood duties. Her bewildered nine-year-old son quickly learned he was not going to get away with reinstituting the patriarchal order of his mother's childhood.

Cleaning bluegill is not a particularly pleasant undertaking. They have needle sharp spines on their dorsal fins and on other fins as well. They also are covered in heavy scales that must be scraped off. Once they are gutted, scaled and the spines and heads removed you end up with a piece of fish that usually fits in the palm of your hand. By the time the fish were ready to cook I had lacerations on both hands that took days to heal. Mom breaded then fried the fish and put them on a large platter in the middle of the dinner table. We eagerly set to devouring the fish only to discover after a couple of bites that we were all picking small bones out of our mouths. While I still felt triumphant in my newfound calling, I was not sure how soon I would bring home another bucket of bluegill.

The solution to that dilemma came only weeks later. For opening day of trout season each April, the California Department of Fish and Game would stock the large pool at the bottom of the Conn Dam spillway with rainbow trout about seven to ten inches long. At first light the pool, maybe forty yards at its widest, would be surrounded by thirty or more young kids like myself and a few adults. We would spend all morning watching our bobbers as they sat motionless for what seemed an eternity but was truly only a few minutes, and then they would plunge under the surface and we would try and hook the fish before it stripped off the worm and left us launching our empty hook, line and bobber back over our heads into the trees behind us. Trout, unlike bluegill, have no sharp spines and at least at this size had no scales, so they were easy to clean. This was more like it. Trout fishing was going to be my true calling. And for most of my life it has indeed remained so, albeit in significantly revised forms over the ensuing decades.

$$****$$

Right: The author as novice trout fisherman.

I soon began exploring the creeks around our home to see if I could find a decent fishing hole. Sarco Creek was not an option as its vernal and spring-fed pools could not sustain fish larger than a couple of inches through the hot summer and fall. But not much further away was a bigger stream, Milliken Creek, which ran year-round and could sustain a range of different fish. I began heading down Monticello Road many mornings with fishing pole in hand. There were fishing holes both upstream and down from the old stone Little Trancas Bridge where Trancas Street met the junction of Silverado Trail and Monticello Road. While the fishing wasn't great, it was more fun than sitting on the side of a glorified rain barrel at Conn Dam where fishing was referred to as "put and take." The Milliken Creek trout were by and large the offspring of steelhead which is a rainbow trout that goes to the ocean for part of its life before returning to spawn in the rivers and streams along the Pacific Coast. Most of the time there were enough of these wild trout to keep me totally engaged.

I gradually ventured further from home, exploring other reaches of Milliken Creek, taking advantage of various friendships made during my time at Vichy Elementary and Silverado Junior High schools. One such friend was Ed Svendsen. My parents would go over to the Svendsen home on a Saturday afternoon for bar-b-que and then play Pinochle with Ed's parents, way into the night. On these occasions Ed and sometimes his younger brother Chuck and I would fish the creek next to their house on Hedgeside Drive. We would fish our way down to a particularly good hole beside his grandmother's house nearby until we had to be back for dinner. Other times I would visit Barry Shaw, another grade school chum and fish the holes below his house on Milliken Creek at Atlas Peak Road. On several occasions during those early years I ventured all the way up the creek towards its headwaters in the Maxwell Ranch area. These were stretches that likely saw few fishermen over the course of a year. Deer and various dry lands wildlife were everywhere. While fishing Milliken Creek I would occasionally watch a belted kingfisher plunge from an overhanging tree into slow moving waters. The foot-long aerial-diver would quickly emerge, fluttering up to a low branch with a three-inch trout in its sharp bill. Beautiful dark blue shoulders and top-notch glistening in the morning sun as it quickly gulped down its catch and then set flight up the river, trailing a taunting cackle in its wake. Most days kingfishers just proved way more adept than I. Within a short distance of my childhood home I increasingly found remote locales where I rarely encountered others, in my mind laying claim to my own natural play land.

The Little Trancas Bridge – photo by Craig Philpott

Many of my trips to Milliken Creek, especially around the Little Trancas Bridge, were devoted not to fishing but pursuing other denizens of the heavily wooded and overgrown creek bed. On one occasion I saw a tiny black tail sticking out between the old roughhewn stones that made up the bridge. The Little Trancas Bridge had been built in 1913 most likely from rock quarried on Mount St. Helena at the northern end of the valley. The original mortar holding the old stones together had begun to crumble in places, leaving gaps between the rocks. I gripped one of the stones just above the space where that black tail protruded. The mortar gave way and I cautiously slid the heavy rock out the side of the structure far enough to see inside. Behind it was a mass of ring-necked snakes, black with orange or yellow undersides and a slender orange ring around their necks. I reached in and pulled out a dozen or more of the eight-to-ten-inch snakes in a single writhing handful. I laughed as I held them with my arm outstretched, like Perseus of Greek mythology holding out Medusa's just-severed head — her hair, as legend has it, a mass of angry serpents. These were far from angry serpents but instead quite docile creatures and did not bite as I gingerly put them back and returned the stone to its place. In hindsight that childhood thrill might be the material of others' nightmares. It seemed to me to be totally in keeping with my near daily adventures along that magical creek.

On other occasions I chased "blue bellies" or western fence lizards that were common to the rocky outcroppings along the creeks. This lizard is also known as a "swift" for reasons that immediately became apparent when I tried to catch one by hand. I could get within a foot or so, but then the lizards darted away faster than my hand could possibly grasp them. But I soon developed an advanced technology for a 9-year-old that solved the problem. I devised a snare out of the end of a stalk of cheat grass. Cheat grass is endemic to grasslands in the Western United States. When it is green it has seed pods growing up a single stem that we would strip off and throw at each other. They would stick in our shirts like little darts. But the green cheat grass stalk also served nicely as a snare. Once I stripped the seed pods off, the remaining 14 to 16-inch stem was both flexible and relatively strong. I would double the slender tip back and tie it in a half knot to the stalk creating a small noose that slid freely along the stem. I could then sneak up on the lizard, slip the noose over its head, and as it darted off the snare tightened and held fast. I would hold the lizard in my hand, marveling at the brilliant turquoise blue of its underside, and then let it go. A slow day of fishing simply gave way to many other wonderful adventures beneath that old stone bridge.

*****

Not long after I had begun my regular treks down Milliken Creek, I discovered the old Water Works above the intersection of Hagan Road and Silverado Trail several hundred yards to the south of the Little Trancas Bridge. There was a beautiful old two-story house with white painted wood siding, hidden in the trees up on the hillside south of the intersection. It was surrounded by woods and immaculately manicured gardens. Lots of flowers and stone walls draped in ivy. Running alongside the old house was a water channel looking ever so much like the Roman-built aqueducts I saw many years later flowing through the Alhambra in Granada, Spain. Less than three feet wide and made of stone, a steady stream, twelve-to-eighteen-inches in depth, coursed through the grounds. In several places it cascaded into small ponds with wooden foot bridges arched over three-to-four-foot-deep pools, then ran down off the property under Hagan Road and further north for a hundred yards or so alongside Silverado Trail before the narrow channel spilled into the confluence of Sarco and Milliken Creeks.

The Water Works was a mysterious place to a young boy. Just up the hill above the old house was a catchment surrounded by cyclone fence topped with barbed wire. Sneaking past the house and up the hillside one morning I reached the fence line and peered through. To my surprise I found a pond teeming with trout. It appeared to be a fish hatchery although no one advertised it as such and there were none of the trappings of a commercial fish rearing enterprise. Behind the pond was a huge stone wall which I later discovered was a forty-foot-high dam built in 1863 by Chinese laborers. Behind the dam there once existed the East Side Reservoir which for a time was Napa's primary water supply. Water was piped into the reservoir from Milliken and Sarco Creeks and then gravity-fed into town. It was supposedly drained and closed after the Second World War, but clearly someone had maintained a small portion of that reservoir to raise trout. It was also apparent from the elaborate fencing that someone did not want either predators or small boys messing with their trout. There was no way I was going to go fishing there. The good news was every so often, particularly after rainstorms, a few of the fish would wash over the screen barrier between the catchment and the water channel below. That meant that if I could sneak onto the grounds, I might catch a fish or two in the little ponds spread throughout the gardens. It was tense going but I never was discovered, and I caught fish on several occasions.

One day I wandered along the ditch below the property as it ran towards Sarco Creek alongside Silverado Trail. I saw trout in various places in no more than 8 inches of water where the ditch could not be more than two feet wide. The trout presumably had washed down from the Water Works in the last storm but had not yet worked their way downstream to the creek. At one point I lay down beside the ditch not five feet from the traffic whizzing by on Silverado Trail, and reached slowly into the water. With my hand open wide I moved ever so gradually up behind a trout and grasped it, pulling my hand up quickly holding the flapping fish high over my prone body. A passing motorist had pulled over on the side of the Trail some yards beyond where I lay. The driver got out and just stared, perhaps thinking I might be an injured pedestrian lying beside the road. But when I raised a brightly colored ten-inch rainbow trout out of the ditch and held it up with a big grin, he just smiled, shaking his head as he returned to his car and drove away. What a kid won't do when left to his own devices.

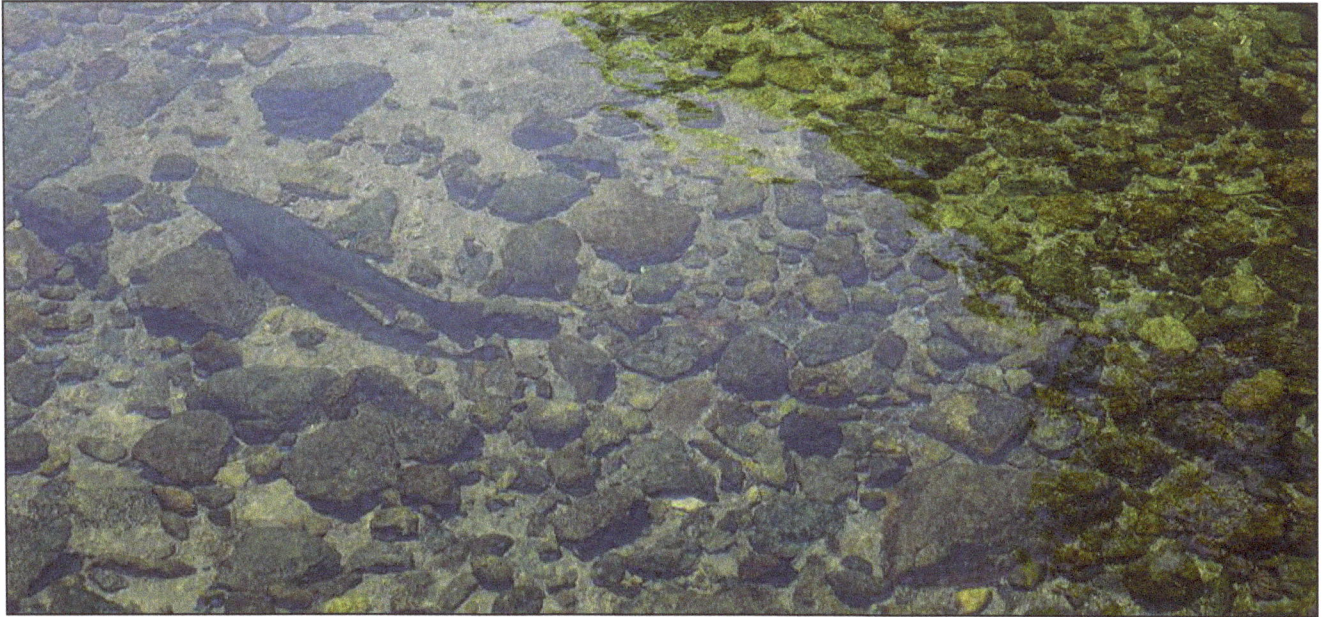

There were infrequent trips outside the Napa Valley in those years that broadened and intensified my immersion in the natural world. When I was fourteen, my parents teamed up with the Guthries and another family, the Blanckenburgs, on one of the most spectacular adventures of my youth. All three families had two children of similar ages, myself and my younger sister Janet, my grade school chum Bruce and his younger brother Roger. Kathy, also my age and who became one of my closest friends throughout my childhood and youth, and her younger brother Ted, were the children of Judge Bill Blankenburg and his wife Mary. One July we rode horses from a ranch west of Bishop up the steep and desolate east side of the Sierra Nevada mountains trailing a train of pack mules over the 11,423-foot Piute Pass. We camped in the Humphreys Basin, a rocky glacial moraine that eventually dropped further westward into the Yosemite Valley. We spent two unforgettable weeks camping above timberline at over 10,000 feet, surrounded by peaks rising to more than 13,000 feet, fishing small glacier cut lakes inhabited by golden trout. But that adventure, and a few in my later high school years, were the extent of my explorations of the larger natural world beyond the valley until I struck out on my own as a young adult. Until then, I engaged nature in all its wonders almost entirely in the rich natural confines of the Napa Valley.

The Sierra Nevada Mountains near Humphreys Basin, as seen from near Bishop, California.

My ensuing forays into the natural wonders of the Napa Valley were guided not so much by fishing as hunting. Like many rural teenage boys of the time, I wanted a gun. No one of course gave even passing thought to handguns in those days. What could you hunt with a pistol? And unless you were going into the further reaches of the hills in the upper valley to hunt the often-scrawny black-tailed deer common to the Northern California coastal region, a rifle made little sense as well. But a shotgun, now there was a gun you could take down to the creeks and across the fields near home and stalk a wide range of prey. It was in the ensuing decade I learned to hunt, to watch for signs of game, to study their habitat and movements. I learned where and during what seasons of the year various birds, including quail, pheasant, doves, ducks and even geese, could be taken.

I started with a simple bolt action 20-gauge shotgun. I would stalk the banks and flood plains of Milliken Creek or the Napa River in sections overgrown by blackberry bushes. Here coveys of valley quail would flush out of the brush as I walked along. Sometimes I would raise a ringed-neck pheasant out of one of the nearby fields. There was a slough bordered by a ten or twelve-foot high levee on either side that ran parallel between Milliken Creek and Silverado Trail where the Trail started north from Trancas Avenue. It was probably a natural channel off the Napa River at the time of the settlement of the valley by non-native farmers in the early 19th century. At some later point the slough was cut off from the river and levees built along its banks, presumably to accommodate wetland conversion to agriculture. By the time I discovered it in the late-1950s it ran for only about a half mile north from the Little Trancas Bridge.

As a novice hunter I would creep up the side of the levee ever so carefully. Peering over the top I would watch the still waters below. If I could see the slightest ripple spreading out from brush or logs along the sides of the slough, I would slide back down the outer levee bank and move slowly up to where I thought the rings were emanating. I would crawl up the levee again, jump up on top of the embankment, and if a duck flew off the slough I would shoot. I probably got no more than one or two ducks in the years I stalked that slough. We called it "jump shooting." But in those endless hours along those levees I learned to watch the way wood ducks would work their way into old hollow trees, or how mallard ducks would drop into a watery opening in the undergrowth of the slough and hide amongst overhanging limbs. "Birder" and Napa founding father E. L. Bickford reported regularly encountering wood ducks starting in 1925 in that same location on the slough after many decades of their absence from the valley, indicating that it has likely been a nesting-ground for those beautiful birds for nearly the last hundred years, and they are likely still there today.

On other occasions I would join my buddy Steve Ceriani at his family's property northeast of Napa in Pope Valley. On early mornings each fall we would walk the dry bed of Pope Creek to hunt mourning doves. The birds would fly by at dawn and dusk at incredible speeds in search of small watering holes, making those hunts some of the most challenging, and least productive, of my youth. Still, the days spent with Steve, who is now deceased, hiking those creek beds or just sitting under a large oak tree and talking about whatever was most pressing on our minds, remain fond memories of my teenage years.

With the onset of high school, I turned my attention more to socializing, girls, sports and from time to time my studies. I still went fishing on occasion with my family, as often as not visiting Pop Guthrie's home in the little town of Westwood near Lake Almanor in the far northern part of California. In winters I would hunt occasionally on the delta region at the northern edge of the San Pablo Bay near where the Napa River entered the Suisun Straits. On very rare occasions I would shoot a duck. But much of the time I would sit in the overgrown edges of wetland areas and watch waterfowl behavior from great distances. I got so I could distinguish the different flight patterns of mallard ducks from pintail sprig and sprig from blue wing teal. I could call in mallards, a call made with the assistance of a small wooden instrument and a sound much like that of a typical barn yard duck. But sprig and teal made very distinct whistling sounds that were impossible to imitate. Teal flew incredibly fast as they zig zagged into ponds to land. I don't recall ever actually shooting one although I no doubt tried. Nevertheless, over those years I developed a keen eye for bird flight patterns at great distances, and bird calls at distances as well.

Early morning at Lake Almanor.

PART 2 – Adulthood and a Return to the Valley

My life in the Napa Valley and my relationship to its natural wonders took a profound turn when I finished high school and a brief stint at the local junior college. I ventured north to Chico State College in 1966 to continue my education. For the next several years I returned to my childhood home mostly during summers. I worked during these periods to pay for my schooling, first working midnight to eight on the graveyard shift at the Kaiser Steel Mill, six nights a week. The following summer I worked as a cub reporter on the Napa Register starting at 5:30 in the morning to make the afternoon deadline, again six days a week. Those long hours working, combined with my limited social life on my few days off, left scant opportunities to return to the nature adventures of my childhood.

Plunging further into adulthood I married my college sweetheart within months of graduating in 1969 and took a job in state government in Sacramento. My incipient career left me with even fewer opportunities to return to my nature haunts in the Napa Valley, although I did occasionally find time to backpack the wilderness areas of Northern California with my wife and friends. After a year I went back to school for graduate studies then returned to my three-piece suit and business lunch lifestyle as a Sacramento bureaucrat, again severely limiting my time in nature. With both my sister and me out of the house, my parents soon moved away from Napa, first to the Bay Area closer to my dad's work, and then upon retirement to the far northern reaches of the state, essentially severing any further ties I had to my childhood home.

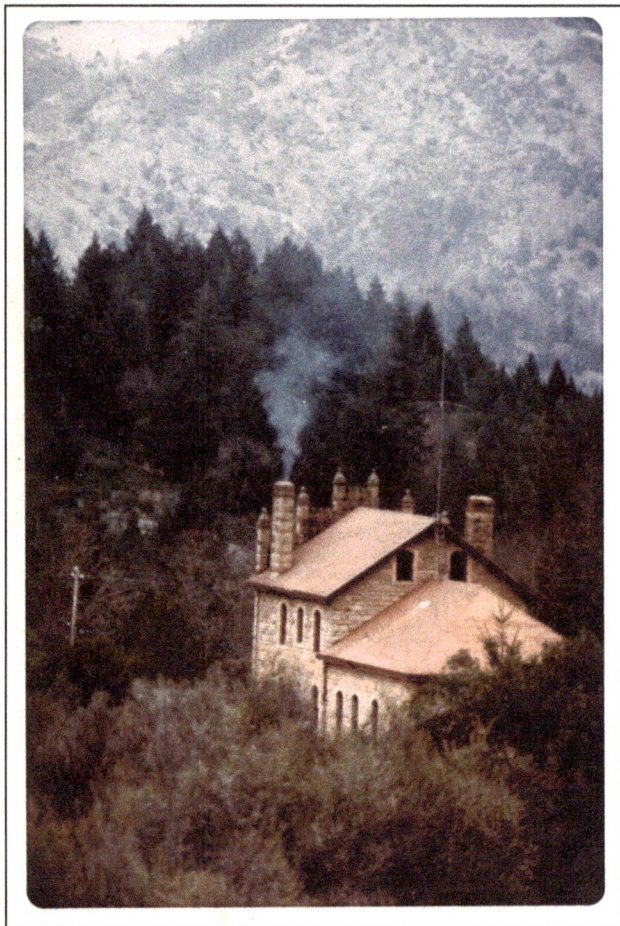

But my pursuit of a relatively traditional path through adulthood soon began to falter. I was successful as a government bureaucrat, and then its appeal began to fade. My marriage was a happy one, and then it too began to unravel. All the while I lived largely separate from the natural world. Eventually it all came apart. One spring morning in 1972 I walked out of my apartment with a backpack stuffed with clothes and a few books, stuck my thumb out on a nearby street corner, and started hitch hiking south. I made it almost to the border between Mexico and Guatemala when several months into my sojourn I became gravely ill while hanging out in a small village on a wild and remote beach in the southern Mexican State of Oaxaca. I returned to the states and after several months recuperating at my parents' house in the Bay Area, I began searching for a place to further recover. Perhaps predictably, although at the time it seemed entirely serendipitous, I returned to the Napa Valley where I found a job as a part-time teacher at the Napa Junior College up valley campus in St. Helena, and a second job as a caretaker for an estate going through probate after the last of the owners had passed away. I moved into a four-story, thirty-room mansion built in 1906 that had fallen into serious disrepair. It was known by locals as Pacheteau's Castle on Diamond Mountain just to the southwest of Calistoga at the very northern end of the Napa Valley. There I quickly rekindled my relationship with the wonderous nature of the Napa Valley and in the process began a much-needed period of healing and both physical and emotional renewal.

The old mansion sat on eighty-five acres of hillside, mostly covered with redwood, madrone, scrub oak and manzanita. Diamond Creek ran nearby and there was also a pond about 100 yards away where I could take a brisk dip on a hot summer day. As I hiked through nearby redwood groves, I was surprised to discover old moss-covered grape stakes standing as ancient sentinels over eroded terraces hidden deep in the heavily wooded hillsides. After a little research I learned this forested mountainside had once been grape vineyards, first planted in 1862, that had been abandoned during Prohibition in the 1920s. I was struck, and encouraged, by the realization that the natural world had reclaimed that land in roughly a half century to the point that only after close inspection could one determine that this seemingly natural area had once been dedicated to commercial agriculture.

Diamond Mountain reaches 2,400 feet at its summit. On several occasions I hiked up from the Castle along the steep hillsides near its top where centuries before early settlers reported huge California condors soaring on updrafts from the valley floor. Once over the top I found large open fields interspersed with densely wooded stands of pine, scrub oak and madrone, in some places giving way to meadows marked by a large solitary live oak as the mountainside sloped westward toward the Sonoma Valley. The mostly undeveloped mountain top was still relatively wild and was home to mysterious and uncommon creatures. One of them was the reclusive pileated woodpecker. It was several times the size of other woodpeckers commonly seen around the valley, roughly sixteen-to-nineteen-inches-tall with a two-and-a-half-foot wingspan (think Woody the Woodpecker on steroids) and a distinct call that could be heard from afar on many a morning's hike. The first time I saw one fly from an old decaying oak tree just up a draw, I was entirely disoriented. Accustomed to the small woodpeckers of my childhood, the large body and wingspan of this woodpecker that otherwise looked like the ubiquitous red-headed woodpeckers of the valley, threw my sense of depth and distance totally off kilter. While I rarely saw one after that first encounter, I was always on the lookout for that shy and unusual inhabitant of the more densely wooded and isolated reaches of Diamond Mountain.

On one of my first hikes up over Diamond Mountain I came upon a small commune made up mostly of potters and their families living in several old buildings in a meadow near the mountaintop. While catching up on the local lore, I was regaled with accounts of a mountain lion recently roaming Diamond Mountain and the occasional eerie screams they heard it make in the night that sounded to them much like the scream of a woman in great distress. As I hiked on through the woods on the back side of the mountain that day, I had occasion to stop, the hair on my arms standing up as I looked around, feeling like I was being watched by that elusive creature. While I never saw a mountain lion on my explorations of Diamond Mountain, I never doubted one was nearby, lurking just at the edge of the senses.

Soon after I moved into the Castle someone broke in while I was away and stole my two shotguns. I had already lost interest in hunting, so it was perhaps fortuitous as I soon picked up a new hobby, photography. Predictably, I was drawn to photographing nature. I bought several lenses appropriate for landscape and wildlife photos, as well as a macro lens which allowed me to photograph minute objects and settings such as light refracting off dew-laden grasses in an early morning meadow, or a tiny mushroom almost invisible to the naked eye, sprouting out of bright green moss on a decaying redwood log. I was exploring nature once again, but from a totally new perspective – nature at the scale of a postage stamp.

I never hunted again. Hunting brought me closer to nature and helped me focus my youthful curiosity on learning the intricate behavior of many creatures and their environs. But as I grew into adulthood, I began to question my relationship to the natural world as one unduly defined by predation. While I remained respectful of the fundamental role hunting plays in the human/nature interface, I found myself drawn more into nature as an observer than a hunter, and in later years, ultimately more as a constituent than observer.

I eventually left the Castle when the estate sold and moved to the east side of the Napa Valley and into another commune, this one in the hills near Angwin off an old dirt tract called Mund Road. The Mund Road Commune was made up of a small group of young adults and various short-to-long term visitors, along with two very young children who came with their single moms. We rented a couple of cottages and a barn turned into a bunk house located on a largely abandoned 640-acre ranch. Here I could explore yet another natural world, one mostly of mazanita and oak, drier than the west side of the valley where redwood stands still flourished. The meadows were again filled with the songs of meadowlarks, along with the cry of red-tailed hawks circling high over the open fields. We boarded horses on the ranch and on occasion I would ride bareback into the hills of the eastern Napa Valley on a gentle but spirited quarter horse of which I grew quite fond. It had been well-trained as a cutting horse although more likely was used for barrel racing or other arena events than as a working horse. I would let it run full out along the dirt roads on the ranch. It would respond perfectly to gentle tugs to its mane or soft-spoken commands, bringing it to a halt from a full gallop without a single side juke or stutter step. We would explore those relatively wild stretches of the upper valley for hours on end. Deer, raccoons, coyotes and the occasional rattlesnake were all part of the daily encounters on my rides through that beautiful side of the valley.

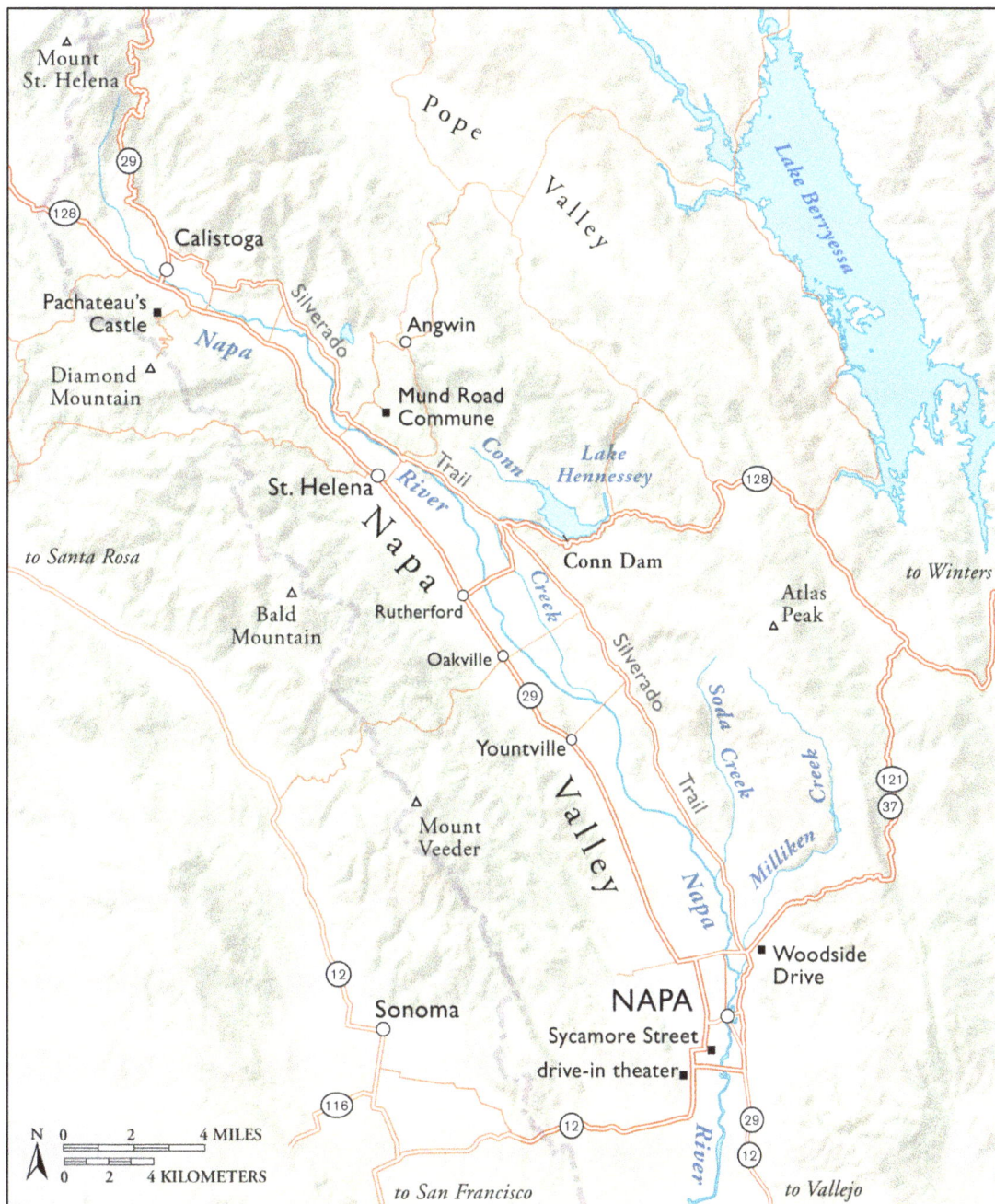

Mount
St. Helena

P o p e

V a l l e y

Lake Berryessa

29

128

Calistoga

Pachateau's
Castle

Angwin

Silverado

Napa

Diamond
Mountain

Mund Road
Commune

Lake
Hennessey

Conn

128

Trail

River

Conn Dam

to Santa Rosa

N a p a

Atlas
Peak

to Winters

Creek

Bald
Mountain

Rutherford

Silverado

Soda Creek

Oakville

29

Milliken Creek

Yountville

121

37

V a l l e y

Trail

Mount
Veeder

Napa

Woodside
Drive

12

NAPA

Sonoma

Sycamore Street

drive-in theater

29

116

12

12

N
0   2   4 MILES
0   2   4 KILOMETERS

to San Francisco

River

to Vallejo

On one occasion I recall vividly, I was walking down a dirt tract that ran in a large circle for about a half mile around a fenced in pasture where the horses grazed. It was a warm late spring morning and I was accompanied by one of the children from the commune, an 18-month-old named David, who was riding atop my shoulders. Just ahead I saw a western bluebird on a fence post. As we walked the bird flew maybe ten feet to the next fence post. Bluebirds will often fly just a short distance away as you approach and if you do not move in a way that frightens them, they will keep a steady distance from you rather than flee entirely. We continued in this little tandem of walk and flight until I put David down beside me and pointed to the bird. "Watch," I said. "It will turn blue." Then holding his hand, we walked forward a few steps and the bird flew to the next fence post. As it did the morning sun caught the bright iridescent blue of its wings and shoulders in a flash of brilliant color. David looked up at me with eyes wide and mouth agape, then pointed and exclaimed, "Boo!" I had a good laugh then put him up on my shoulders again and proceeded on our morning stroll. The bluebird continued to flutter ahead from post to post. David, totally enthralled, would shriek Boo! Boo! giggling unabashedly as only young children can, each time the bird flew. That was the first time I recall thinking to myself – you know, I might really enjoy being a dad someday. Nearly two decades later I did have a son, and as I suspected on that beautiful morning stroll along that large open meadow, it has become a most wonderful dimension to my life, for now over 30 years. Daniel, my son, is more of an urban creature than his dad, but his love of the natural world is strong and growing.

The author and David strolling with the bluebirds

PART 3 – You Can't Go Home Again

Still, I remained restless and after another year or so left the Napa Valley again, this time only to return for a few brief visits, never for more than a day or two. Years began to pass between visits, then decades. But with each ensuing visit the truth in Thomas Wolfe's famous book title, *You Can't Go Home Again*, became ever more apparent. The Napa Valley of my childhood and young adulthood is now, nearly a half century later, rapidly disappearing. Within a one-mile radius of my childhood home, the transformation has been profound. Gasser's large prune orchard has been pulled up and replaced by vineyard planted in Cabernet Sauvignon grapes which produce wine sold at upwards of $200 and $300 a bottle and for which the Napa Valley is now famous the world over. The large open meadow I wandered through when I ventured over that back fence in my childhood is now an extension of that same vineyard, turning my childhood's magical kingdom into a half mile wide sea of grapes from Monticello Road all the way to Sarco Creek. Milliken Creek has gone through striking changes as well. The wild upper reaches of the creek on the Maxwell Ranch near Atlas Peak have long since been turned into the exclusive Silverado Country Club, with some of my favorite fishing areas repurposed as putting greens and water traps. The old stone Little Trancas Bridge where I fished, hunted and learned so much about the natural world, is now a permanent homeless encampment with the natural wonders I discovered there giving way to the desperation of the most marginalized of modern society. The old Water Works just down the road a few hundred yards now stands in stark contrast to the homeless encampment. Where I once surreptitiously searched for fishing holes through rambling gardens, woodlands and waterways now stand large private luxury homes behind gated drives, part of what has become one of the most expensive real estate markets in the world.

The upper valley where I spent those wonderful few years in recuperation and renewal as a young adult in the 1970s has changed no less dramatically. That hillside behind the Castle above Calistoga with its moss-covered grape stakes and eroded terraces beneath a forested overstory has again been cleared and terraced as it was in the 19th century, rededicated to growing wine grapes. The Castle has become one of several small boutique wineries on the mountainside and Diamond Mountain a terroir of the highest order. The ridgelines that surround the upper end of the valley are now frequented daily by brightly colored, shiny gliders towed above mountain tops by airplanes from the nearby Calistoga airport. They now catch those same thermal updrafts rising from the valley floor that were frequented by California condors nearly two centuries before.

I suspect that reclusive pileated woodpecker I encountered so infrequently has now disappeared entirely from the mountain. Perhaps the mountain lion has gone the same way.

But if you can't go home again, neither can your childhood home be far from the life it engendered. In the nearly half century since I left the Napa Valley I have lived in and traveled across many parts of the world. I have explored the jungles and tropical rainforests of Latin America and East Asia, and the savannas and bush country of southern and eastern Africa. I have fished, scuba-dived, free-dived and snorkeled many spectacular reefs and oceans from the Caribbean to the South China Sea, from the Sea of Cortez to Zanzibar, from the Hawaiian Islands to the Pacific Coast of Central America, and more. In a sense, each adventure has been just another extension of those early excursions into the natural world on the outskirts of the Napa Valley of my youth.

Over the past several decades I have made my home in Northern Colorado. It is another place of natural beauty where almost daily I ramble over a range of many thousands of acres of woodlands, fields, rocky bluffs, canyons and river that are part of a large multi-use land trust known as the Phantom Canyon Ranch. Photography has fallen victim to failing eyesight, and fly fishing has all but succumbed to the indignities of aging as well. Hiking remains the central feature of my near-daily immersion in something much grander than myself. With each passing decade I have found myself more a part of the natural world than an observer, and far less the seeker of nature's conquests of my youth. Gazing up at the Milky Way on those spectacularly clear Colorado nights, absent the ever-present light pollution that most of us endure unawares, I am increasingly conscious of not only from whence I came but more importantly of that of which I am but a most minuscule constituent element. As I venture out tomorrow over another back fence, I will be reminded again that the warp and weft that is the fabric of my life is in large part held together by a single thread that began nearly three quarters of a century ago in a bygone Napa Valley.

Author's mountain retreat, Phantom Canyon Ranch

Author and son descending into the Phantom Canyon.

More about the author:

Douglas L. Murray is Professor Emeritus, Department of Sociology, Colorado State University. He has published extensively on international development, agriculture, health and the environment, including *Cultivating Crisis: The Human Cost of Pesticides in Latin America.* Austin: University of Texas Press, 1994; and *Fair Trade: The challenges of transforming globalization.* London and New York: Routledge, 2007; with co-editors Laura T. Raynolds and John Wilkerson. He has been a John D. and Catherine T. MacArthur Foundation Research and Writing Fellow in the Program on Peace and International Cooperation, and a Fulbright Senior Research Fellow. He is currently working on the second in a series of natural history memoirs, *In Search of the Paper Nautilus - Life is a Beach Afterall*, while relishing self-isolation in his mountain retreat on the Phantom Canyon Ranch. For communication with the author send email to dmurray@colostate.edu

Acknowledgements:

With gratitude to Michael Crane, Cathy Mathews, and Ed Svendsen for their fact and memory checking, and to my wife, Robin Mitchell, for her patience and loving care.

www.ingramcontent.com/pod-product-compliance
Lightning Source LLC
Chambersburg PA
CBHW042354030426
42336CB00029B/3477